ralfjones250@gmail.com
951-403-4275

PRAISING GOD
FOR OUR
INTELLIGENT DESIGN

A Thirty-One-Day Devotional

Ralford Jones, Ed.D., Psy.D.

WESTBOW
PRESS®
A DIVISION OF THOMAS NELSON
& ZONDERVAN

WestBow Press books may be ordered through booksellers or by contacting:

WestBow Press
A Division of Thomas Nelson & Zondervan
1663 Liberty Drive
Bloomington, IN 47403
www.westbowpress.com
844-714-3454

ISBN: 978-1-6642-2790-3 (sc)
ISBN: 978-1-6642-2792-7 (hc)
ISBN: 978-1-6642-2791-0 (e)

Library of Congress Control Number: 2021905603

Print information available on the last page.

WestBow Press rev. date: 08/17/2021

To my grandchildren Cameron and Ava, and the friends who encouraged me to put my thoughts I shared with them through texting, into a devotional. I praise, honor, and thank God my Creator for the insights, prompting, and sustenance of health through the writing process. Also, I celebrate God's creative genius and superintelligence for designing and creating every part of my body.

CONTENTS

INTRODUCTION

God created us for His glory – Isaiah 43:7. One aspect of this obligation is for us to glorify God for and with our whole body. Worshiping God is a 24/7 experience - I Corinthians 10:31. Some Christians create a false distinction between their secular and spiritual lives; this text is unsupportive of such separation. Everything God's faithful followers do is in the Spirit and not worldly according to Romans 8:9.

Worship is essential to our existence. Our utmost worshipful experience comes when we love God with our entire being – Mark 12:30-31. The utilization of the different parts of the body in glorifying God is an essential theme of this devotional. Utilizing the total emotional, mental, and physical capabilities might be a new concept or experience for some individuals. However, if the Spirit guides them, this comprehensive worship involvement stimulates enthusiasm, freshness, and spontaneity in their devotions.

Why a thirty-one-day devotional? This devotional encourages consistent practice to foster psychological transformation. It's a popular belief that it takes 21 days to develop or break a habit. Dr. Maxwell Maltz, a plastic surgeon in the 1950s, observed that it took some individuals at least 21 days for old mental images to disappear and for new ones to solidify. However, other scientific observations show that some habits took a shorter or much longer time to form or eliminate.

The universal knowledge is uncontested that it takes us humans, some time to develop and destroy psycho-emotional and behavioral patterns, tendencies, and practices. This devotional provides the readers with consistent exercise to glorify God for and with different parts of their bodies for 31 days. Under the guidance of the Holy Spirit, these practices develop new neural networks that reinforces such habits. I pray that this will be your experience.

DAY 1

KEEP YOUR HEAD HIGH

"Keep your head up. God gives His hardest
battles to His strongest soldiers."
—Anonymous

Ralford Jones, Ed.D., Psy.D.

BODY FACTS

The head is considered the most crucial part of the body. It is the control center of your system. The head houses the primary sensory organs of the body, chief of which is the brain. The senses of sight, hearing, smell, and taste come from the head.

The head can bow, nod, shake, shout, and sing in worshipful movements. Some of these gestures at church might be uncomfortable for you. Private home devotions can provide the freedom for such expressions. If you devote your head to God, He can transform it into a praise machine. Have a functional plan to give God all the worship (adoration, gratitude, obedience, praise, and reverence) you can give with your head. **Get ready for three devotions on the head.**

KEEP YOUR HEAD HIGH

"But you keep your head in all situations, endure hardship, do the work of an evangelist, discharge all the duty of your ministry" (2 Timothy 4:5 NIV).

God strategically designed your head for worship. Therefore, keep it sober. Sobriety is indispensable for effective worship. A sober head is not an incidental occurrence but an intentional pursuit aided by divine assistance.

The phrase "keep your head" is transliterated by some Bible translations as – "be sober-minded," "exercise self-control," "be serious," and "be vigilant." This last phrase was Paul's encouragement to his young friend Timothy. We also need this type of spiritual sobriety and vigilance. Paul used the word sober or self-controlled more frequently than other New Testament writers. He encouraged his listeners to "think with sober judgment" (Romans 12:3 ESV). He advised the church leaders and older men to be sober-minded and self-controlled (Titus 2:2 and 1 Timothy 3:2). Paul recommended that the Holy Spirit, not wine, should intoxicate Christ's followers (Ephesians 5:18 KJV).

Paul's messages in Galatians 5:21 and Titus 2:11–13 broaden the understanding of sobriety beyond inebriation and link it to salvation. Sobriety involves moderation, putting aside worldly passion, and living a godly life. Sobriety also includes intentional reflection and purposeful living in anticipation of Jesus's Second Coming.

Praise God generously today for and with your head. Think about sobriety and wear a color to represent it, as an act of worship. When you stay spiritually sober, you are glorifying God. If you lack soberness, God can download temperance and moderation into your brain. Today, expand your worship repertoire – bow, nod, and shake your sober head in praise to God. May God keep you clearheaded always.

Ralford Jones, Ed.D., Psy.D.

DEVOTIONAL REFLECTION

1/1/23

Do you spend time learning how God can use your head to honor Him and bless others?

Tatiana - no
Me - yes always singing songs, watching videos, reading the bible

Why does God want you to be sober, and what is your approach to achieve and maintain sobriety?

Tatiana - to be more intuned & understand his word. Me - So I can be filled with him and him alone.

Are you efficiently using your head to fulfill God's purpose for your life?

Tatiana - I am not
Me - No, I can do more

How can you give more honor to God for your head?

Tatiana - I don't know
Me - Open my mouth and pray aloud

Write some additional thoughts about your head as a praise machine.

DAY 2

BLESSINGS COVER THE HEAD

"Well, you do have all those gray hairs." I point to the few silver
strands coming through.
"They're not gray," Mom barks at me as she opens her
door. "They're strands of glittery goodness."
—Margaret McHeyzer

Ralford Jones, Ed.D., Psy.D.

BODY FACTS

Hair is mainly amino acid, the building block for the tough protein known as keratin, found in vertebrates' teeth and skin. Each strand of hair has three main parts. The shaft is the visible part that grows out above the skin. The follicle holds the hair in the skin. The base of the follicle is known as the hair bulb, which contains living cells.

God knows how many strands of hairs are on our head – Matthew 10:30. An average head consists of about 100,000 follicles. Despite their colors, length, and textures, head hairs are blessings from God.

BLESSINGS COVER THE HEAD

"Blessings are on the head of the righteous, but the mouth of the wicked conceals violence. The memory of the righteous is a blessing, but the name of the wicked is not" (Proverbs 10:6–7 BSB).

Position your head in God's direction! God has some special blessings that you need. Philippians 4:8 provides clear instructions on such positioning –focus your thoughts on spiritual things.

Proverbs 10:6–7 contains two contrasting ideas in the same sentence. This literary approach is known as an *antithesis*. These verses focus on the blessings of the righteous and the fate of the wicked. The correct interpretation of the "Blessings on the head of the righteous" is the conferral of answered intercessory prayers by God.

Scientific knowledge and common-sense experiences confirm that benedictions are on our heads. Head hairs protect us from ultraviolet rays, deadly insect bites, bruises, and scratches; they also regulate body heat during hot and cold temperatures. Head hairs can also change one's appearance making one looks fierce, casual, formal, beautiful, or handsome.

Not only is one's original natural hair a blessing, but Proverbs 16:31 notes, "Gray hair is a crown of splendor, it is attained in the way of righteousness" (NIV). According to Proverbs 20:29, gray hair is something magnificent for chronologically mature individuals. These texts contradict the popular modern view that gray hair should be hidden and feared. God has a positive view of gray hairs, and He wants us to understand that growing older should be embraced gracefully.

Pray and honor God with and for your head today. Imagine God answered your silent intercessory prayers for someone's healing. Also, imagine that your happy mood changes your brain wave patterns, causing the alpha and beta waves to glorify God.

DEVOTIONAL REFLECTION

If you have hairs on your head, how many things about them can you see as God's blessings to you?

_____

_____

_____

What are your thoughts about the scripture that says gray hairs are blessings from God?

_____

_____

_____

Does God actually know the number of hairs on each person's head?

_____

_____

_____

How can you enjoy your hair more despite its texture, color, length, and amount?

_____

_____

_____

If you have hair, write your thoughts about its texture, color and length.

_____

_____

_____

DAY 3

THE ULTIMATE BLESSINGS FOR THE HEAD

"One who wants to wear the crown, bears the crown."
—Lee Min-ho

BODY FACTS

The head is the seat of intelligence, and God has crowned our heads with wisdom, knowledge, understanding, high intelligence, commonsense, skills, and numerous talents. Let us praise God profusely for the functioning of our heads.

Today is another opportunity to think and stay outside the box with your praise to God for creating your head.

THE ULTIMATE BLESSINGS
FOR THE HEAD

"There is reserved for me in the future the crown of righteousness, which the Lord, the righteous Judge, will give me on that day. . . to all those who have loved His appearing" (2 Timothy 4:8 HCSB).

God knows the measurements of your head! If you are faithful like Paul, God will place your custom-made crown on your head.

The British monarch, Queen Elizabeth II, was crowned on June 2, 1953, at age twenty-five. For that grand coronation, the Imperial State Crown, made of gold, silver, platinum, ruby, and sapphire, was adjusted for her perfect fitting. If you are faithful to God, He will place the most expensively designed crowns on your heads on 'coronation day.' "I am coming soon. Hold fast to what you have, so that no one will take your crown" (Revelation 3:11 BSB).

The Bible mentions crowns as rewards for God's faithful children. When Paul wrote 2 Timothy 4:8, he probably was in prison awaiting his gruesome execution. However, he looked beyond his situation and location into the future and envisioned Jesus rewarding his dedication with a Crown of Righteousness. The recipients of this crown will only be righteous individuals.

James 1:12 mentions a Crown of Life that God will give to those who triumphed over their trials and were consistent in their love for Him. According to Revelation 2:10 (ESV), the faithful ones will receive the crown of life. "Be faithful unto death, and I will give you the crown of life."

I Peter 5:4 speaks of the Crown of Glory. The message indicates that this crown will maintain its luster, and Jesus, the Chief Shepherd, will award it. Like Paul, I am looking forward to my diadem. Are you?

Reflection on eternity allows your prefrontal cortex to replace cortisol, the stress hormone, with oxytocin. Visualize and feel this love juice making your heart and mind more loyal and loving to God. May you thank God abundantly today for and with your head!

Ralford Jones, Ed.D., Psy.D.

DEVOTIONAL REFLECTION

Visualize God placing the Crown of Righteousness on your head, then describe the virtual experience.

_____

_____

_____

Why is the same crown described in three different ways in the Bible?

_____

_____

_____

What can you do to protect your head from injuries and make it healthier?

_____

_____

_____

How can you show more gratitude to God for your head?

_____

_____

_____

Write any additional thoughts regarding the devotional thoughts on the head.

_____

_____

_____

LET GOD TRANSFORM YOUR THINKING

"I consider that a man's brain originally is like a
little empty attic, and you have to stock
it with such furniture as you choose. Now
the skillful workman is very careful
indeed as to what he takes into his brain attic."
—Arthur Conan Doyle

Ralford Jones, Ed.D., Psy.D.

BODY FACTS

The brain has two hemispheres. The left is more dominant in creative activities, such as visual and performing arts. The right shows preferences for analytical and logical activities such as mathematics and sequential quantitative reasoning. The hemispheres work together very well. The brain is responsible for our awareness, imagination, intelligence, judgment, memory, thinking, and more.

When the righteous brain creates new pathways, heals itself, and grows, it is worshiping God. One of the most important and conscious ways to honor God for your brain is to keep it healthy. So, it can think clearly, plan effectively, retain and recall information adequately, process information at a reasonable speed, and support the other parts of the body interdependently. **Get ready for a four-day exciting trip with the brain.**

LET GOD TRANSFORM
YOUR THINKING

"Do not be conformed to this world, but be transformed by the renewal of your mind, that by testing you may discern what is the will of God, what is good and acceptable and perfect" (Romans 12:2 ESV).

Your brain is trapped! If it's not giving God the praise, He deserves and requires for creating your cerebellum. Be bold and creative with your worship so God can modernize your brain into a full-fledged praise machine.

Romans 12:2 has three important messages. The first is a directive that addresses the relationship between Christians and the world. This command comes as a strong warning against adopting worldly behaviors and customs. According to 1 John 2:15–17, if a person loves earthly things, God's love is absent in him/her. This text places worldly stuff into three categories: the lusts of the flesh, the desires of the eyes, and the pride of life.

The second message of Romans 12:2 is a directive for transformation by adopting a new mindset. This process is futile without God, who can radically change our minds to experience new perceptions, emotions, and behaviors. God can effect immediate epigenetic changes in our lives by switching some of our genes on or off. God can rewire our brains' circuitry to quickly develop new neural networks that generally take months or years.

The third message is a challenge to critically evaluate the things we encounter so that we can identify God's virtuous, attractive, and faultless plan for our lives. Jerimiah 29:11, 3 John 1:2, 1 Timothy 2:4, 1 Thessalonians 5:16–18, and John 13:34 note that God desires us to prosper, be in good health, be saved, pray continually, and always rejoice in Him, be sanctified, and love one another deeply.

Research shows that frequent concentration on God's love, while praying and meditating changes people. Their prefrontal cortex becomes more active over time to reduce distractions, increase attention, love intentionally, and have the desire to forgive. May you glorify God for and with your brain today.

Ralford Jones, Ed.D., Psy.D.

DEVOTIONAL REFLECTION

What are your strategies for overcoming conformed thinking that is harmful to your relationship with God?

_____

_____

_____

Is your worship experience very creative?

_____

_____

Are you adequately fulfilling God's purpose for your brain?

_____

_____

_____

How often do you praise and thank God for your brain?

_____

_____

_____

What transformation needs to occur in your life?

_____

_____

_____

THE HERCULEAN TASK

"A mind without control is like an airplane without a joystick.
It's bound to crash."
—Bhavesh Chhatbar

Ralford Jones, Ed.D., Psy.D.

BODY FACTS

The pons connects the cerebrum and cerebellum to the spinal cord and regulates our wakefulness, sleep, breathing, blood pressure, consciousness, and heart rate.

Today you have another opportunity to use the power of your brain to praise, honor, and appreciate God for your mind. Choose a victory color and wear it in thankfulness to God for disciplining your mind.

THE HERCULEAN TASK

"We demolish arguments and every pretension that sets itself up against the knowledge of God, and we take captive every thought to make it obedient to Christ" (2 Corinthians 10:5 NIV).

Your errant thoughts are your greatest enemy. When they are messing up your relationship with God. Managing and restricting the freedom of your thoughts, extricating their defiance, and subjecting their will into obedience to Christ, is a Herculean task, only possible with divine assistance.

Here are four ways to achieve this obedience. First, believe in and apply Philippians 4:13 (NIV): "I can do all this through Him who gives me the strength." God can enable us to subject all our thoughts to His obedience. Second, follow the instruction of 2 Corinthians 10:4 (NLT): "We use God's mighty weapons, not worldly weapons, to knock down the strongholds of human reasoning and to destroy false arguments." Paul presented several weapons for spiritual warfare; 2 Corinthians 6:7 highlights righteousness as a powerful armament. Romans 13:12 (NIV) speaks of "the armor of light," and Ephesians 6:13–18 presents the whole armor and "praying continuously in the Spirit."

Third, acceptance of the Holy Spirit's power can give us supremacy over our thoughts. John 14:12–17 presents Jesus instructing His disciples on empowerment through prayer, faith, and the Holy Spirit. Here Christ revealed that His disciples would accomplish more extraordinary things than He achieved by utilizing the Holy Spirit's power. Our brains would be more potent if the Holy Spirit controlled them. The fourth approach combines faith and prayer as a formidable weapon for spiritual warfare. Matthew 21:21-22 shows the power of faith and prayer, and Ephesians 3:12 alludes to the effectiveness of faith and prayer.

Thank God repeatedly today for and with your thoughts. Such practice and mindfulness can develop mental stamina. Intentional resistance of wayward thoughts, and immediate gratitude to God, for victory, can empower the brain for future resistance. May these worshipful actions, make you more spontaneous to resist the devil and obey God.

Ralford Jones, Ed.D., Psy.D.

DEVOTIONAL REFLECTION

Share your thoughts on 2 Corinthians 10:5.

_____

_____

_____

How successful have you been in bringing your bothersome thoughts under control?

_____

_____

_____

Do you honor God sufficiently for your reasoning ability?

_____

_____

_____

What one thing do others share about your thinking ability that you appreciate?

_____

_____

_____

Write any additional thoughts you have regarding today's devotional reading.

_____

_____

_____

GOD REWARDS THE WISE WITH KNOWLEDGE

"We must not be wise and prudent according to the flesh.
Rather, we must be simple, humble, and pure."
—Francis of Assisi

Ralford Jones, Ed.D., Psy.D.

BODY FACTS

God created the brain as a very delicate and sensitive organ. Consequently, He designed unique protective environments to provide for its safety. These include the hard skull, three tough layers of membranes, and fluid that fills the extra protection spaces.

Only an intelligent creator could think of these protections, not nature.

GOD REWARDS THE WISE
WITH KNOWLEDGE

"The simple believes everything, but the prudent gives thought to his steps. The simple inherit folly, but the prudent are crowned with knowledge" (Proverbs 14:15, 18 ESV).

God's generosity is mind-blowing! God gives more than meets the eyes. So, get ready for His showers of blessings.

Proverbs 14:15 and 18 show the intellectual functioning of two individuals: the simple and the prudent. The word *simple* is the English translation for the Hebrew word *peti; it* means credulous or readily believing something without evidence. The text presents two essential things regarding the simpletons. One, their inherited folly could be a generational problem, influenced by their genes or environments. Two, they can be victimized easily by misinformation and the devil's ploys.

The foolish or simple individuals are described in James 1:8 as double-minded and unbalanced in their ways. God is willing to reduce or eliminate whatever foolishness we acquire if we work consistently with Him. According to James 1:5, those who lack knowledge can petition God, and He will generously distribute it without finding faults.

The Hebrew word for *prudent* is *waarumin*, and it means wise, intelligent, and sensible. The main text shows that wise individuals are thoughtful before making decisions, and God rewards them with knowledge. According to Ecclesiastes 7:12 (ESV), "the advantage of knowledge is that wisdom preserves the life of him who has it."

Shout, *'praise God,'* for your brain! Imagine, your oscillating brain waves are also coordinating their patterns in a call and response sequence in praising God. May you wear a color for wisdom in thankfulness to God for His insights.

Ralford Jones, Ed.D., Psy.D.

DEVOTIONAL REFLECTION

What are some of your insights into Proverbs 14:15 and 18?

_____

_____

_____

How can you honor God more appropriately for His wisdom imparted to you?

_____

_____

_____

How are you positioning your brain to be drenched with God's wisdom, knowledge, and understanding?

_____

_____

_____

In what activities are you frequently engaged to become wiser?

_____

_____

_____

Why does God want us to have the package of wisdom, knowledge, and understanding?

_____

_____

_____

DAY 7

VERTICAL INTEGRATION OF THE MIND

"Positive thinking can achieve the impossible."
—Vijay

Ralford Jones, Ed.D., Psy.D.

BODY FACTS

The hypothalamus is very important for balance, controlling hormone secretions, and awareness of the temperature, hunger, and thirst.

Many of us often take our brains for granted, and we sometimes operate for days forgetting that we have one. Be aware that the primary purpose of your brain is to worship God.

VERTICAL INTEGRATION OF THE MIND

> *"Come now, let us reason together, says the Lord: though your sins are like scarlet, they shall be as white as snow; though they are red like crimson, they shall become like wool"* (Isaiah 1:18 ESV).

It is common knowledge! God operates on a different intellectual plane and spiritual frequency than humans. Therefore, take full advantage of this fantastic invitation.

God's thoughts and ways transcend ours, and we are incapable of understanding and calculating this distance accurately. Isaiah 55:9 notes, "As the heavens are higher than the earth, so are my ways higher than your ways and my thoughts than your thoughts" (NIV). Irrespective of these geographical, spatial, and spiritual differences, God desires us to reason with Him. Acceptance of this invitation exposes us to vertical transcendent thinking, perpendicular understanding, and linear reasoning at a supreme spiritual level. This vertical integration will send God's spiritual signals into our brain waves so we can operate on His frequency.

Philippians 4:8 (KJV) presents a disciplined approach to keep our thoughts on God's frequency: "Finally, brethren, whatsoever things are true," honest, just, pure, lovely, "of good report; if there be any virtue, and if there be any praise, think on these things." Paul's insights offer a life-changing experience achievable by new spiritual experiences, different mindsets, and deep meditative thinking that align with God's thoughts. Then we will become truthful, honest, just, pure, lovely, and a reporter of good news. Unfortunately, the deep contemplative focus and consistent commitment required to achieve these characteristics are often not appreciated or practiced by some Christians.

Close your eyes and visualize God coming to reason with you. Focus on His posture, listen to the dialog, look at His eyes, and experience the connection. Then praise and honor God for this incredible experience.

Ralford Jones, Ed.D., Psy.D.

DEVOTIONAL REFLECTION

How often do you reflect or meditate on the things mentioned in Philippians 4:8?

_____

_____

_____

What does it mean to reason with God?

_____

_____

_____

Think of some areas of your brain and their functions and thank God for them. What parts come to mind?

_____

_____

_____

How much have you enjoyed focusing on the brain for the past four days?

_____

_____

_____

Write any additional thoughts you have regarding today's devotional reading.

_____

_____

_____

DAY 8

YOUR EYES CAN TRANSMIT CHRIST'S LIGHT

"Let my soul smile through my heart and
my heart smile through my eyes,
that I may scatter rich smiles in sad hearts."
—Paramahansa Yogananda

Ralford Jones, Ed.D., Psy.D.

BODY FACTS

The eyes are avenues to the soul. When a light ray enters the cornea, it bends the ray to pass easily through the pupil to the retina. The light then becomes light impulses that pass through more than one million nerve fibers, and then it is sent to the brain via the optic nerve and interpreted as images by the brain.

God created your eyes to worship Him. Think how much your eyes have allowed you to see and accomplish. The eyes can see, blink, cry, read, stare, wink, and closed in prayer to God. What about wearing a color to represent your eyes for the next four days. Throughout, be mindful that this act is thanking and praising God for your eyes. **Let your eyes twinkle for the following four devotions.**

YOUR EYES CAN TRANSMIT CHRIST'S LIGHT

"The eye is the lamp of the body. So, if your eye is healthy, the whole body will be full of light, but if your eye is bad, your whole body will be full of darkness. If then the light in you is darkness, how great is the darkness" (Matthew 6:22–23 NIV).

God made your eyes for more than sight. Whenever the light of Jesus penetrates your eyes, it automatically transforms you into a translucent and transcendent being. Therefore, let Jesus's light enter your retina so others may observe your transformation and glorify God.

Jesus's profound message in Matthew 6:22–23 speaks of the importance of the eyes for physical and spiritual health and illumination. If the eyes are unable to transmit light, the body is engrossed in gloom and wickedness. The Bible is an excellent source of light because it is God's instructions that enable us to live godly lives. The Holy Spirit can transform God's word into illuminative and practical applications – becoming wiser and more obedient.

John 1:9 describes Jesus as the authentic light who shares His brightness with everyone. John 8:12 (ESV) is a transferal declaration from Jesus, intended to brighten our paths. "I am the light of the world. Whoever follows me will not walk in darkness, but will have the light of life." The acceptance of Jesus's lifestyle illuminates and elevates us for responsibilities. Matthew 5:14–16 (NIV) calls us to be bright lights to the world by letting others see our illuminations: "Instead, a lamp is placed on a stand, where it gives light to everyone in the house."

Thank God for what you accomplished with your eyes. Observe some beautiful flowers and praise God. Stare at the sunset and thank God with raised hands. Glare at the word LOVE in John 3:16 and contemplate God's deep love for you. Gaze at your eyes in the mirror and be grateful for their intricate design. May your eyes' worship, catch God's attention.

Ralford Jones, Ed.D., Psy.D.

DEVOTIONAL REFLECTION

If you can see, you have numerous reasons for which to thank God. Reflect on some of these reasons and write a thank-you note to God.

_____

_____

_____

What actions are you willing to take so you can become more knowledgeable about your eyes?

_____

_____

_____

What actions are you taking to protect your eyes and make them healthier?

_____

_____

_____

How can you use your eyes to transmit God's love?

_____

_____

_____

Write down some unique ways your eyes can praise God.

_____

_____

_____

VISUAL STIMULATION ELICITS WORSHIP

"Early summer evenings, when the first stars come out, the warm glow of sunset still stains the rim of the western sky. Sometimes, the moon is also visible, a pale white slice, while the sun tarries. Just think—all the celestial lights are present at the same time! These are moments of wonder – see them and remember."
—Vera Nazarian

Ralford Jones, Ed.D., Psy.D.

BODY FACTS

The cones of the eyes are primarily responsible for seeing colors. The cones have three photopigments: blue, green, and red. The reflected light from a yellow surface can activate the green and red cones, which send signals to the optic nerve and the brain to interpret the color we are seeing.

God is an awesome Creator! His ability for details is unrivaled.

VISUAL STIMULATION
ELICITS WORSHIP

"The heavens proclaim the glory of God, and the sky above proclaims his handiwork" (Psalm 19:1 ESV).

Suppose you took your eyes and sight for granted. It would be best to revolt against your nonchalant and unappreciated attitude. More than 49 million people worldwide are blind.

If you can see in colors, God is responsible for implanting rods and cones in the receptor cells of your retinas so that you can see the rainbow. If you failed to be exuberant in praising God for the ability to see, be brave and protest against your carefree approach. Because one in 30, 000 individuals has total color blindness – a syndrome known as achromatopsia.

Psalm 119 is David's response to the visual stimulation he experienced. This verse honors God for His creation of the celestial bodies and celebrates the gift of sight. David saw beyond the mere twinkling stars of a clear midnight sky; he recognized God's glorious fingerprints all over the sky. In Psalm 97:6, David proclaimed God's righteousness and glory when he saw the heavens. Like David, God expects us to praise Him eloquently when we see His beautiful works.

Some individuals are impressed mainly by grandeur or exquisite beauty. They often overlooked many beautiful things and people that are considered ordinary. You can train your mind and eyes to see the beauty in every flower, bird, or tree if you are such a person. Start by believing that God does not create ordinary things or people.

Think of the different ways your eyes are fulfilling God's purposes for your life and thank God for His blessings. Blinking cleans the surface of your eyes with tears so the images the retina receive can be brighter. If you have dry eyes, get the right product and lubricate them. For a week, cook and shop for your eyes by buying them nutrients and protection. These worshipful actions can help your whole body. May God grant you the audacity to praise Him uniquely with your eyes.

Ralford Jones, Ed.D., Psy.D.

DEVOTIONAL REFLECTION

If you can see colors, you are blessed; many individuals cannot. For this blessing, praise and honor God by writing a short prayer to Him.

_____

_____

_____

It is easy to take your eyes and sight for granted. Write some things you will do to be more focused on the blessings you see and be more thankful for the experiences.

_____

_____

_____

What have you seen recently that impressed you to worship God?

_____

_____

_____

In what ways are you using your eyes to fulfill God's purpose for your life?

_____

_____

_____

Write any additional thoughts about today's devotional thoughts.

_____

_____

_____

USE THE LIDS WISELY

"A covenant made with God should be regarded
not as restrictive but as protective."
—Russell M. Nelson

Ralford Jones, Ed.D., Psy.D.

BODY FACTS

Light reflects when we look at someone, and the brain interprets the light in useable ways. Two individuals can see the same person or thing, and their interpretations of who or what they saw can be different due to their perceptions or how the brain sorts the information.

Use your eyes to read God's words so they can be a lamp to your feet.

USE THE LIDS WISELY

"I made a covenant with my eyes not to look lustfully at a young woman" (Job 31:1 NIV).

Put a lid on it! This action will protect you like Job and preempt specific lustful desires. Do you have a visual protective approach like Job?

God created our eyes with lids to manipulate voluntarily, and He desires us to use them wisely. Overexposure of our eyes to unhealthy stimuli is retinal abuse, and God will hold us accountable. When in doubt about the rated contents of the visual bombardments you experience, put a lid on it unapologetically. Here's a mantra for your eyes – "Turn my eyes from looking at worthless things" (Psalm 119:37 ESV).

God made our eyes to see His beautiful creation and resemblance in others so that we would treat them as His children. These purposes are to help accomplish God's plans and goals for our lives. Job was an avant-garde who had many inventive ideas to keep himself spiritually focused and grounded. No wonder God boasted about his uniqueness. "Have you considered My servant Job? For there is no one on earth like him; he is blameless and upright, a man who fears God and shuns evil" (Job 2:3 NIV). God wants to applaud you also for your faithfulness.

Job's covenant suggests that he understood Jesus's amplification of the law. He also knew that his eyes were windows and avenues to his soul. Job's unique contract is profound; it's a progressive approach for successful spiritual living. Job's contract contributed to his decency, nobility, and reverence for God. Like Job, make it a priority to control the visual images that can potentially derail your spirituality.

Say, *thank you, God, for my eyes!* Close and shut your eyes and listen to the sound they make. See if you can put the sound into a tune. Imagine that your eyes' automatic blinking and silent sound are their natural ways of praising God. May you use your eyes creatively to praise God today.

DEVOTIONAL REFLECTION

What are your thoughts about Job making a covenant with his eyes?

_____

_____

_____

Below, please draft a covenant for your eyes.

_____

_____

_____

What special things some people do to protect their eyes and make them healthier?

_____

_____

_____

Do you believe that your eyes are the avenues to your soul?

_____

_____

_____

Write any additional thoughts you have pertaining to today's devotion.

_____

_____

_____

PULL THE SHUTTERS DOWN

"Somehow, you need to cling to your optimism. Always look for the silver lining. Always look for the best in people. Try to see things through the eyes of a child. See the wonder in the simplest things. Never stop dreaming."
—Richie Sambora

BODY FACTS

Opened eyelids distribute tears over the surface of the eyes. Closed eyelids block out light rays and enhance sleep.

Many children are good at closing their eyes when they see embarrassing things on TV. Many adult Christians should model this approach when they see something that can challenge their spirituality.

PULL THE SHUTTERS DOWN

"I will not look with approval on anything that is vile. I hate what faithless people do; I will have no part in it." (Psalm 101:3 NIV).

Your eyes can be obstacles to your spiritual growth! Don't let them steal your blessings. Manage your eyes well to reflect God's image, absorb wisdom and knowledge, and fulfill His purpose in you.

Like Job, David understood the eyes' power and the necessity to control what he saw. David vowed to disapprove of the things that were base, evil, vulgar, worthless, or wicked. This approach was functional and practical for David. He knew that uncontrolled and unfocused eyes could create a torrent of spiritual discombobulation: infidelity, an illegitimate birth, murder, and a cover-up scheme. David's message is more than a personal vow or contract; it is a promising approach to those who have spiritual challenges with their eyes. In our permissive and amusingly filled society, it is easy for many Christians to seek the visual fulfillment of carnal desires. If you are traveling down this road, stop and reflect on Romans 8:7.

Knowledge of your eyes' natural tendencies for certain attractions is essential for spiritual guidance and success. Ignorance regarding the visual images that distort thinking, deregulate emotions, and negatively influence behaviors amounts to be careless, foolish, and spiritually dangerous conduct. Unfortunately, your eyes cannot avoid all spiritually harmful contents. However, when you have these inadvertent experiences, God expects you to look away, cover your eyes, take another route, censor, rebuke the visuals, and bring the shutters down. We can also call on God's name immediately for support because He is a present help in troublesome times.

Your eyes are highways to your soul; honor God for and with them. Use your eyes to search and find hope and encouragement in scripture. Also, place your eyes to see things that stimulate glorious and reverent thoughts. May God use your eyes today to transmit His love and kindness.

Ralford Jones, Ed.D., Psy.D.

DEVOTIONAL REFLECTION

Whether you can see or not, thank God for the wonderful images you can see or visualize.

_____

_____

_____

What visual stimuli you encounter that concern you, and what steps have you taken to address the issue?

_____

_____

_____

Would it be necessary to write a commitment to God to keep your eyes from unholy contents?

_____

_____

_____

Do you know someone you care about who is having difficulties with pornography? Would you be willing to share David's approach with this person?

_____

_____

_____

Were the devotions on the eyes beneficial to you?

_____

_____

_____

AN IMPORTANT REMINDER

"God gave people two ears and one mouth because He
wants us to listen twice as much as we talk."
—Joshua Harris

BODY FACTS

The external ear is about eight to ten millimeters in diameter and has three parts: the flap or pinna, ear canal, and eardrum. The pinna channels the sound through the ear canal and causes the eardrums to vibrate.

God created your ears to worship Him and to accomplish His purpose. The ears are avenues to the soul; we should use them prudently to hear and listen to the voice of God, the beautiful sounds of nature, and the inspiring words of other humans. You can use your ears in unconventional ways to enjoy worshipping God. **There are four days of excellent reading for your ears.**

AN IMPORTANT REMINDER

"The hearing ear and the seeing eye that see, the Lord has made them both" (Proverbs 20:12 ESV).

Perchance you have forgotten! Here's a friendly reminder. God is the Designer and Creator of your ears. Use them wisely.

The first part of Proverbs 20:12 is an apothem – a truism. Here are some possible implied messages that it is communicating. The ears are for hearing and are to be used for this purpose. We should be careful what we choose to hear and listen to our messages, just as we expect others to receive them. If God created the ears, He is capable of hearing our faintest cry. Listening to God should be a priority for our ears because He owns them, and we are the stewards.

Good use of our ears involves listening to God and giving auditory attentiveness to others. According to Luke 1:41, 44 (ESV), "When Elizabeth heard Mary's greetings, the baby leaped in her womb, and Elizabeth was filled with the Holy Spirit." Mary's greeting influenced two powerful reactions. First, the unborn baby moved energetically. If good news caused an unborn child to leap, it must be a powerful stimulus. Second, the Holy Spirit occupied Elizabeth. Our greetings can bring excitement to others and sanction the presence of the Holy Spirit.

Here are two salient messages on listening for us to heed. "My dear brothers and sisters, take note of this, everyone should be quick to listen, slow to speak. . ." (James 1:19 NIV). "To answer before listening – that is folly and shame" (Proverbs 18:13 NIV). If one listens before speaking, this can demonstrate intelligent behavior.

Sing and clap praises to God for your ears if you can, and fill them with melodious worshipful content for the day. Then think about the contributions your ears made to your successes and spiritual satisfactions. Sit and enjoy some quiet time later; you might hear God's message. May you position your ears to listen to God.

Ralford Jones, Ed.D., Psy.D.

DEVOTIONAL REFLECTION

What are the blessings of your ears for which you are most thankful?

_____

_____

_____

How can you use your ears to honor God more?

_____

_____

_____

Are you a good listener?

_____

_____

_____

Name somethings you enjoy hearing.

_____

_____

_____

Write any additional thoughts about today's devotion.

_____

_____

_____

THE SYNCHRONISTIC ACTIONS

"Assuming that what we hear does not contradict the scriptures, this is how we learn to hear the Lord, by doing what we think we hear then seeing what happens."
—Marcia Lebhar

Ralford Jones, Ed.D., Psy.D.

BODY FACTS

About five percent of the world's population – 466 million adults and children have disabling hearing loss.

If you can hear clearly with or without an hearing aid, be generous with your praise to God for such ability. Today let your ears itch or have this longing desire - to hear God's voice or words.

THE SYNCHRONISTIC ACTIONS

"Therefore, everyone who hears these words of mine and puts them into practice is like a wise man who built his house on the rock" (Matthew 7:24 NIV).

Your ears can make you wise! "Tune your ears to wisdom" (Proverbs 2:2, NIV) and "Incline your ear and hear the words of the wise" (Proverbs 22:17, NIV).

Hearing and listening might not be synonymous. Hearing is the physical and automatic process that allows sound to enter the ears. Listening is an essential aspect of hearing that includes intentionality, perception, and understanding a message. Doing involves practical obedience and devotion to God. When you synchronize your actions with what you heard from God's Word, it will give you eternal life, John 5:24.

The message of Matthew 7:24 is a synchronism of hearing and doing. The background of this setting is Matthew 5:3–7:23. Jesus and His disciples sat on a mountainside, and a large crowd gathered below. The first messages Jesus delivered were the eight beatitudes. Throughout these three chapters, Jesus addressed more than thirty topics, and some individuals had difficulty digesting and understanding some of the meanings. The synchronism of hearing and doing is a progressive way to praise God for the ability to listen.

God desires His children to be wise, so He made the ears to facilitate this process. The ability to hear God's messages and put their contents into action is a blessing that increases wisdom. This same approach activates faith. According to Romans 10:17, faith comes from hearing God's Word. James 1:5–6 notes that God gives wisdom generously when we asked and believe. Christians' ears can worship God constantly because their hearts and ears seek and acquire knowledge (Proverbs 18:15).

Thank God repeatedly for your ears! Throughout today, say the word BELIEVE, from Acts 16:31, so your ears can hear the vibrating sound. May this simple act of worship confirm your belief in the power of God to save you.

DEVOTIONAL REFLECTION

Do you believe the level of appreciation you have for your ears determines how much you honor God for their design and functioning?

_____

_____

_____

Are you having difficulties with being obedient to God's requirements?

_____

_____

_____

How can you praise God more for the design and functioning of your ears?

_____

_____

_____

Are you experiencing difficulties with your hearing? If so, write a prayer to God for healing. If not, write a prayer to God to thank Him for your well-functioning ears.

_____

_____

_____

Have you tried moving your ears like you playing an accordion, if so, what song did you play?

_____

_____

_____

THE RECIPROCAL
EXPERIENCE

"For the things we have to learn before we can
do them, we learn by doing them."
—Aristotle

BODY FACTS

Here are three general information reminders regarding the ears and hearing. The average ear size is approximately two inches long. The ear is an anatomical body part that grows longer as an individual gets older. Hearing loss is also associated with age.

Express your gratitude to God for the wisdom he gave to the individuals who developed and keep improving hearing aids.

THE RECIPROCAL EXPERIENCE

"Whatever you have learned or received or heard from me or seen in me – put it into practice. And the God of peace will be with you" (Philippians 4:9 NIV).

Be a practitioner of God's Word! It will prompt God to show up at your address, hang out with you, and bring His gift of peace.

Philippians 4:9 is a reciprocal text that requires us to listen and obey. When you move from hearing to doing, you transcend your basic spiritual functioning to a deluxe upgrade where you can enjoy God's peace. Obedience to God always activates His blessings. They might be delayed, disguised, or packaged differently than expected, but these personal blessings are custom-made and given timely. Deuteronomy 28:1–2 suggests that God responds favorably to diligent obedience.

Romans 10:17 (NIV) is another hearing and doing reciprocal text: "So faith comes from hearing, and hearing through the Word of God." Hearing and faith work together intimately to make our Christian experiences purposeful and rewarding. This partnership is worth cherishing. When this verse combines with Hebrews 11:6 and Ephesians 2:8, it provides a remarkable spiritual sequence – Hearing produces faith, faith makes it conceivable to believe in God's existence, and belief in God makes salvation possible.

When Jesus was departing to heaven, He delivered to His disciples these reassuring words: "Peace I leave with you; my peace I give to you. . ." (John 14:27 ESV). There is a dissonance when one hears and believes but disobeys what is heard. Obedience however, removes this cognitive dissonance, provides harmony, and chases fear, anxiety, and worry.

Be creative in praising God for and with your ears. Use them like an accordion. Hold each lobe with your thumb and index finger and pull and push them sideways repeatedly. Let the index fingers press against the tragus and listen to the sound. You can create a rhythmic pattern of a simple mantra or song – *'Thank you Jesus, thank you Lord!'* May you enjoy this unique worship experience.

Ralford Jones, Ed.D., Psy.D.

DEVOTIONAL REFLECTION

Record your understanding of Philippians 4:9.

_____

_____

_____

Is there a biblical imperative you have difficulty following? If so, why?

_____

_____

_____

How does God use hearing and faith to enhance your spiritual growth?

_____

_____

_____

Have you ever heard God's audible voice? If so, share your experience?

_____

_____

_____

Write a thank-you note to God for allowing your ears to be involved in your salvation.

_____

_____

_____

THE ZONE OF COMPASSION

"Listening is such a simple act. It requires us to be present
and that take practice but we don't have to do anything
else. We don't have to advise or coach, or sound wise.
We just have to be willing to sit there and listen."
—Margaret J. Wheatley

BODY FACTS

The ears house the three smallest bones. The malleus, incus, and stapes are in the middle ear. The ossicles are like a bridge between the outer and inner ears.

God designed the ears to worship Him, and He causes them to function with much efficiency.

THE ZONE OF COMPASSION

"Whoever shuts their ears to the cry of the poor will also cry out and not be answered" (Proverbs 21:13 NIV).

Position yourself for a reciprocal blessing! Know where to hear the legitimate cry of the poor. Then remove the ribbon from Proverbs 28:27 and listen to the chiming of your gift.

The book of Proverbs has many relevant messages regarding the proper treatment of the poor. Proverbs 21:13 presents a stern warning that echoes throughout the Bible: there are consequences for ignoring the poor's legitimate cries. Some individuals describe this effect as bad karma. Many Christians perceive this cause and effect dynamic as a divine consequence. According to the implied message of this verse, our attentive God will answer the needs of those who respond appropriately to the poor's concerns. "Whoever gives to the poor will not be in need, but he who hides his eyes will receive many curses" (Proverbs 28:27, BSB).

This message has another dimension – Proverbs 19:17 (ESV): "Whoever is generous to the poor lends to the Lord, and he will repay him for his deed." When we loan something to the Lord, He gives a far better return than any financial institution. It is often effortless to be kind to the poor without getting emotionally involved with them. We are urged by 1 John 3:17 (ESV) to connect with the poor. The deep love for everyone that I Peter 4:8-10 speaks about is for the poor also. According to Hebrews 13:16 (ESV), God is pleased with our kindness: "Do not neglect to do good and to share what you have, for such sacrifices are pleasing to God."

Worship God for and with your ears today! Take deliberate action to listen with understanding to a poor person's genuine needs. Then let God impress you to respond appropriately. Today, let the word GIVETH, from Proverbs 28:27, frequently ring in your ears. May you receive God's blessings, because you heard what the poor needs and act dutifully.

Ralford Jones, Ed.D., Psy.D.

DEVOTIONAL REFLECTION

How do you usually respond to the needs of the poor?

_____

_____

_____

Before someone gives to the poor, should they think about why they are in such a predicament?

_____

_____

_____

Please contemplate how God can use the needs of the poor to bless us.

_____

_____

_____

How can the cry of a poor person be the sound of God?

_____

_____

_____

Do you think it is necessary to emotionally connect with the beggars on the street?

_____

_____

_____

A STRONG RESOLUTION

"When doubt comes against us, we have to lift up the shield of faith. We do this when we open our mouth and say what God's Word says, rather than grumbling and complaining about the problem."
—Joyce Meyer

Ralford Jones, Ed.D., Psy.D.

BODY FACTS

The mouth is called the buccal cavity; it begins at the lips and ends in the back of the throat. The two main sections of the mouth are the vestibule and the oral cavity. The vestibule is the zone between the teeth and cheeks.

God designed and created the mouth primarily to glorify Him. God deserves the utmost oral articulation and declaration of praise, gratitude, and love for designing and creating our mouths.

The mouth can pray, comfort, complain, counsel, curse, eat, motivate, play instruments, praise, preach, speak, sing, shout, teach, yell and eloquently communicate. Think of the importance of your mouth to your health, success, spirituality, and relationships. **Get ready to be blessed, because four devotions on the mouth are next.**

A STRONG RESOLUTION

"You have tried my heart; you have visited me in the night. You have tested me in the night. You have tested me and found no evil; I have resolved not to sin with my mouth" *(Psalm 17:3 BSB).*

It is worse than stinky breath. The unconverted mouth destroys friendship, embarrasses its owner, and makes one's religion worthless. God can clean up the filthiest mouth and transform it into a fountain of continuous praise.

Resolved is a robust word that means determination, the strength of will, decisiveness, or firmness of purpose. David recognized that his mouth was very challenging to control. Consequently, he resolved to manage it properly. According to Psalm 17:4, David avoided evil people and trusted God's commands. Psalm 39:1–4 shows five ways David kept his mouth from sinning. One, he watched his ways. Two, he muzzled his mouth when he was close to the wicked. Three, David refused to speak. Four, he meditated. Five, he focused on his mortality. Although David broke his silence later, the utterance of his mouth was pure.

If you are in a situation where it is difficult to restrain your tongue, use David's strategies. In Psalm 19:14, David used meditation to help him think before speaking. David prayed that his verbal utterances and meditations would please God. Psalm 1:1–2 declares that those who frequently meditate on God's Law will be blessed. David often meditated on God's law until it became part of his spiritual DNA. More Christians would experience emotional, mental, and spiritual benefits if they practiced this type of meditation.

Sing praises and gratitude to God today with and for your mouth. How can you praise God continually with your mouth like David – Psalm 34:1? In every situation, be thankful, move your tongue when quietude is required, and pray continuously – in good and challenging times, during pleasure or pain, when working, and throughout every conscious hour. May your mouth brag about God's goodness always.

DEVOTIONAL REFLECTION

Are you using your mouth sufficiently and efficiently to praise God for its design and functioning?

_____

_____

_____

Can you write a resolution today not to sin with your mouth?

_____

_____

_____

What strategies have you used in difficult situations to muzzle your mouth?

_____

_____

_____

Why do many individuals have difficulty restraining their mouths?

_____

_____

_____

Do you have a unique way to praise God with your mouth?

_____

_____

_____

GUARD YOUR MOUTH

"Be sure to taste your words before you spit them out."
—Anonymous

Ralford Jones, Ed.D., Psy.D.

BODY FACTS

The mouth is part of the breathing mechanism. When the mouth works cooperatively with the teeth and tongue, they aid with speech and eating.

God created our mouths to praise Him, and He is skillful to use them to fulfill His purposes for our lives. The enjoyment that the mouth gives, its benefits to our physical survival and financial achievements, and its opportunities to speak and bless others give us thousands of good reasons to honor and praise God for it.

When last have you whistled? I have not done so for donkey years and attempted last week and could not. Now, after a week, I'm almost back to my teenage years. Based on the chorus of "Jesus loves me, this I know," I whistled this to my granddaughter, and she loves it. *Thank you, Jesus, for my nose, thank you Jesus for my toes, thank you Jesus for my heart, thank you Jesus for all parts.* I had fun with this praise chorus.

GUARD YOUR MOUTH

"Lord, set a guard for my mouth; keep watch at the doors of my lips" (Psalm 141:3 CSB).

Don't sweat over this enormous responsibility. God made your mouth. He understands its behaviors and knows how to manage it efficiently and consistently.

In Psalm 39:1, David seemed self-assured that he could watch and muzzle his mouth and avoid sinning with his tongue. That was David before he sinned with Bathsheba and arranged her husband's death. In Psalm 141:3, David showed humility when the prophet Nathan confronted him for his atrocities. David's prayer recognized his inability to control his mouth, thus giving God complete control. David framed his request in military-like language; he wanted soldiers to guard and watch over his lips, and if something slipped by before fully uttered, another layer of armed protection on the inside would muzzle his tongue.

Our best effort in managing our mouths will fail miserably sometimes. Therefore, all Christians need Jerimiah's experience: "And the Lord said to me, behold, I have put my words in your mouth" (Jeremiah 1:9 ESV). God's word is the best guard for our mouths; let's chew and digest it daily. Some Christians have large vocabularies that need replacing with an oasis of fresh, flavorful, and fortifying words.

Here is Paul's assessment of the unconverted human mouth: "Their throats are open graves; their tongues practice deceit. The poison of vipers is on their lips. Their mouths are full of cursing and bitterness" (Romans 3:10–19 NIV). This cavity is incapable of keeping its heart's secret; it speaks before the brain thinks, embarrasses itself, and ultimately self-destructs. Proverbs 13:3 says that those who guard their mouths conserve their lives.

Today is an excellent time to glorify God for and with your mouth! Conceptualize eating as a flavorful and delectable worship experience. Imagine blessing and slowly chewing the food; this pulverizes the molecules, distributes the flavors to interact with the saliva, and incites the tastebuds to dance joyfully. May your mealtime be a worshipful occasion.

Ralford Jones, Ed.D., Psy.D.

DEVOTIONAL REFLECTION

How can you use your mouth to honor God and uplift someone today?

_____

_____

_____

How can you allow God to control your mouth daily?

_____

_____

_____

What are the things about your mouth for which some changes are needed?

_____

_____

_____

Do you know someone who is having difficulty controlling his/her mouth?

_____

_____

_____

What suggestion could you give this person to exert more control?

_____

_____

_____

SILENCE CAN BE GOLDEN

"Focus your attention on the quality of your words, and
not the quantity, because few sensible talks attract millions
of listeners more than a thousand gibberish."
—Michael Bassey Johnson

BODY FACTS

Our oral cavity has a mucus membrane that contains saliva glands, and the fluid it produces keeps our mouths moist. This moisture softens and helps with food digestion and makes swallowing easier. Though mainly water, saliva also contains antibacterial substances, electrolytes, and enzymes.

God seems to include everything necessary for the mouth to function well when He created it. When last have you clapped your tongue? I just started practicing it with my chorus - *Thank you, Jesus, for my nose, thank you Jesus for my toes, thank you Jesus for my heart, thank you Jesus for all parts.*

SILENCE CAN BE GOLDEN

"Too much talk leads to sin. Be sensible and keep your mouth shut" (Proverbs 10:19 NLT).

Do not lose your focus! Keep track of the number of words you speak. You are the quality and quantity control manager of your mouth. Remember, "A word fitly spoken is like apple of gold in settings of silver" (Proverbs 25:11 ESV).

Proverbs 10:19 refers to foolish individuals' communication style as lacking understanding, foresight, and judgment. These individuals demonstrate carelessness and idleness in their speech, often sharing unsubstantiated information or gossip. In 2 Timothy 2:16 ESV, Paul encourages Timothy to "avoid irrelevant babble, for it will lead people into more and more ungodliness."

In Matthew 6:7, Jesus taught that His followers should not babble like the pagans, who believed that long prayers would get their God's attention. Jesus did all the praying for our sins in Gethsemane so we could enjoy short ones. Long prayers are often repetitive; this meandering is not spiritually productive.

Luke 18:10–14 (NIV) presents a parable of two men, a Pharisee, and a tax collector, who went to pray. The Pharisee had a lengthy prayer that included boasting and self-righteousness. The tax collector's prayer was simple: "God, have mercy on me, a sinner." Jesus noted that the taxpayer went home more justified than the Pharisee.

When one prays to God, the prayer should be reflective and short, according to Ecclesiastes 5:2. When we are hasty in speaking to God, this hurried prayer can become a monologue; the same is true of long prayers. God wishes to dialogue with us daily; we should give Him and ourselves this opportunity to enjoy quality time together.

Hum a tune thanking God for your mouth. Research shows that humming reduces pain and stress, lowers blood pressure, vibrates brain cells, calms the body, enhances sleep, produces nitric acid, and releases oxytocin. Humming is an effective worship tool to access God's blessings; please use it effectively. May you use your mouth creatively to increase your worship repertoire.

Ralford Jones, Ed.D., Psy.D.

DEVOTIONAL REFLECTION

God has given you another day to eat and speak! How can you uniquely use your mouth to thank Him for these blessings?

_____

_____

_____

Deeply contemplate Proverbs 25:11 and write your reflection.

_____

_____

_____

How can too much talk become sinful? Should more humming be incorporated in public and private worship?

_____

_____

_____

What strategies can you use to make your communication with God and others more effective?

_____

_____

_____

Do you think the normal length of your prayers need adjusting?

_____

_____

_____

A FOUNTAIN OF LIFE

"You can change your world by changing your words.
Remember, death and life are in the power of the tongue."
—Joel Osteen

Ralford Jones, Ed.D., Psy.D.

BODY FACTS

The tongue is a muscular organ that enables us to speak. It can often indicate if we are sick or healthy. An average adult tongue has about 10, 000 taste buds that are replaced around twice monthly. The number of taste buds is reduced based on age. Our tongues have four separate taste zones: sweet, salty, sour, and bitter.

Every time you taste something enjoyable and healthy, get excited and acknowledge God for creating the four zones of your tongue.

A FOUNTAIN OF LIFE

*"The mouth of the righteous is a fountain of life, but the mouth
of the wicked conceals violence" (Proverbs 10:11 NIV).*

Watch your mouth! Be careful that your conversations are not stale,
boring, and lifeless! God wants to use your mouth to speak life into
death and dying situations. Dedicate your mouth to God, and He will
use your conversations to heal, comfort, and inspire others.

The first part of Proverbs 10:11 highlights how our mouths can
fulfill God's purpose for our lives. Unfortunately, some believers of
God adopt unsavory rhetoric of hatred, prejudice, unkindness, and
racism. God calls Christians to supply the world with words of truth,
encouragement, hope, peace, and love.

Be aware that the natural tendency of your mouth is to spew vile
words. In Romans 3:10-19 (NIV), Paul presents the actual condition of
the human mouth. "Their throats are open graves, their tongues practice
deceit. The poison of vipers is on their lips. Their mouths are full of
cursing and bitterness."

Listen to the converse in Colossians 4:6 (NIV): "Let your
conversation be always full of grace, seasoned with salt, so that you
may know how to answer everyone." A well-seasoned meal is delightful
and satisfying, just like wholesome conversations. Some people have
perfected the art of bland, ugly, or crude speech; they embrace the
ideas that jokes must be vulgar to be enjoyed. God frowns at this belief.
Ephesians 5:4 speaks against filthy language, foolish conversation, and
coarse jokes. God wants your mouth to produce cascades of fresh,
naturally clean, elevating, refreshing, and life-giving words.

Shout *glory hallelujah* for your mouth! Use your mouth to recite, sing,
or whistle the first half of Proverbs 10: 11. This devotion will send
much worshipful content to your creative brain cells. Picture these cells
running and dancing with the information and producing more creative
ideas. May your mouth create fresh, honest, and cheerful conversation
always.

Ralford Jones, Ed.D., Psy.D.

DEVOTIONAL REFLECTION

How can your mouth be a fountain of life?

_____

_____

_____

Are you struggling with jokes and crude remarks that Paul warned against?

_____

_____

_____

Are your conversations generally seasoned with love and truth?

_____

_____

_____

Is your mouth fulfilling God's purpose for your life?

_____

_____

_____

Are you willing to increase your vocabulary to make your prayers more interesting and effective?

_____

_____

_____

WORSHIP GOD WITH YOUR BEST EFFORT

"God has given us two hands, one to receive
with and the other to give with."
—Billy Graham

Ralford Jones, Ed.D., Psy.D.

BODY FACTS

God designed our arms and hands with three major nerves. These nerves control our hands' muscles and enable them to experience tingling sensations, touch, pain, and temperature. More than any other part of our bodies, our hands are the most productive in making things, completing chores, and manually helping others.

Think about all the blessings your hands accomplished and what your life would be without them. God made our hands to build things, clap, cook, garden, hug, lift, massage and caress, pull, pick and pick up things, play games and instruments, wave, touch, write, etc. For such flexibility and agility, God deserves high marks and lots of praise for His ingenious design and creation. Make it a regular habit to praise and thank God for your arms and hands! **Get ready for three exciting hand devotions**.

WORSHIP GOD WITH YOUR BEST EFFORT

"Whatever you find to do with your hands, do it with all your might, for in Sheol, where you are going, there is no work or planning or knowledge or wisdom" (Ecclesiastes 9:10 NIV).

Your hands can be a lethal weapon! When used without divine guidance. Therefore, use them cautiously and intelligently to dispense love.

The command of Ecclesiastes 9:10 presents a motivational approach to work that involves strength and energy. Dr. Martin Luther King Jr. captured the essence of this message in a speech entitled *What Is Your Life's Blueprint?* Dr. King eloquently articulated that if one's job is to sweep streets, one should perform this responsibility like Beethoven composing music, Michelangelo painting pictures, and Shakespeare writing poems.

Ecclesiastes 9:10 suggests that God's influence should guide our activities. If the heart and mind are unconnected to God, work can be just an opportunity to receive a paycheck, and performance could be mediocre. God is challenging us to move from mediocrity to excellence. When we give our best to small tasks, God will bless us with more significant opportunities. The author encourages us to evaluate our performances and operate in a zone of optimal performance. Research showed that our health and overall well-being are enhanced when we work in this zone.

Conversely, functioning in the low-performance zone creates anxiety and health issues. Remember, God's watchful eyes are in your direction, looking for occasions to bless you. The text is associated with an expiry reason – we will die. John 9:4 reminds us to do God's work while we have life because all work ceases at death.

Today, give God a rousing hand praise, in love and appreciation for creating your hands to accomplish so many good things. Imagine that this clapping is the exclusive content of your 20 minutes worship. God made your hands to praise Him and to fulfill His purpose for your life. So, be generous with your hand praise. May your clapping, waving, and saluting honor the King of Kings.

Ralford Jones, Ed.D., Psy.D.

DEVOTIONAL REFLECTION

Is it a regular habit of yours to thank God specifically for your hands?

_____

_____

_____

How can you use your hands to meet the challenges of Ecclesiastes 9:10?

_____

_____

_____

Are your hands generally operating in a high-performance zone?

_____

_____

_____

Has your mortality ever been a motivator for your performance?

_____

_____

_____

What hand praise are you comfortable giving God for creating your arms, palms and fingers?

_____

_____

_____

GOD CAN USE WHAT'S IN YOUR HANDS

"I have held many things in my hands, and I have lost them all;
but whatever I have placed in God's hands, that I still possess."
—Martin Luther

Ralford Jones, Ed.D., Psy.D.

BODY FACTS

Each of our hands has twenty-seven bones. The wrist has eight bones arranged into two equal rows. Touching and holding hands can decrease the stress hormone cortisol and increase oxytocin, the feel-good hormone.

Praise, honor and thank God meaningfully and regularly for your hands' superb design and fantastic functioning.

GOD CAN USE WHAT'S IN YOUR HANDS

"Then the Lord said to him, "What is that in your hand?" "A staff," he replied. The Lord said, "Throw it on the ground." Moses threw it on the ground and it became a snake, and he ran from it" (Exodus 4:2–3 NIV).

What's UP? The message of this text is Utilization and Power. God can utilize your hands with His power to heal and fulfill His purpose for your life. The same power that animated Moses's staff can transform the inanimate things you use daily, such as a computer, phone, or pen, to bless others.

You probably know the story, how God surprised Moses by transforming his staff into a snake. This miracle bolstered Moses's confidence and credibility before Egypt's Pharaoh. God can use your hands more supernaturally than a stick.

Moses was a descendant of Abraham. When Abraham's grandson Joseph became prime minister of Egypt, God used his creativity to distinguish him as a very successful leader. After the deaths of Joseph and the Pharaoh who promoted him into the leadership position, Joseph's relatives grew in great numbers, and the Egyptians became fearful and enslaved them. God responded to the Israelites' cries for deliverance and chose Moses to be His spokesman and liberator.

Exodus 4:2–3 presents at least four pertinent lessons: First, God's questions and commands are important and require obedience. Second, obedience to God's request should supersede our perceptions and astonishments. Third, God can use anyone or anything to achieve extraordinary accomplishments. Fourth, some transformations can be rapid, like Moses's staff.

Bless the name of the Lord for and with your hands. Plan your worship in the kitchen sometimes. Use your hands to chop/cut, grate, knead, mix, pour, stir, or wash your food as you focus on Ecclesiastes 9:10. Be intentional in cooking a delicious and healthy meal. These cooking activities are creative forms of worship. May God use your hands for something spectacular today.

Ralford Jones, Ed.D., Psy.D.

DEVOTIONAL REFLECTION

When was the last time you really focused on the design and usefulness of your hands? If you did lately, please share your experience or discovery.

_____

_____

_____

How can you use your hands to praise and honor God?

_____

_____

_____

Do you think God deserves more praise from you for the creation and functioning of your hands?

_____

_____

_____

How would you like God to transform your hands like He did with Moses's rod?

_____

_____

_____

Would you allow God to use your phone, pens, and or computer to help others?

_____

_____

_____

KEEP YOUR HANDS CLEAN

God has given us two hands—one to receive with and
the other to give with. We are not cisterns made for
hoarding; we are channels made for sharing.
—Billy Graham

Ralford Jones, Ed.D., Psy.D.

BODY FACTS

Five fingers seem the perfect amount for our palms. The forearm controls the tendons in the fingers. Our fingers can indicate if we have health issues such as anemia, blood circulation and oxygen level problems, and mineral deficiencies. The receptors on the fingers transmit messages to the brain.

Do something creative with your hands regularly to worship God for their intricate design and usefulness. Do you know that there are many spiritual or health benefits for raising your hands? Raise hands above your head can improve posture and increased deeper breathing. It strengthens shoulders and arms. Raising hands can improve balance. It also strengthens the spine and legs. After a meal, it helps food move faster through the large intestine.

KEEP YOUR HANDS CLEAN

"He that hath clean hands, and a pure heart; Who hath not lifted up his soul unto falsehood, and hath not sworn deceitfully. He shall receive a blessing from Jehovah, And righteousness from the God of his salvation" (Psalm 24:4–5 ASV).

Are your hands clean? If they are, don't mess them up. This predicament could forfeit your salvation.

Clean hands contribute to good physical health, especially as a protective measure against the COVID-19 virus. This cleansing involves – thorough soaping of the hands and washing with warm running water for at least twenty seconds. While this virus is very deadly, sin is more fatal. Knowing how to clean our hands spiritually is essential, because our salvation depends on this knowledge.

Psalm 24:3 poses an important question regarding the requirements for ascending to God's holy place. The answer in verse four is not referring to ceremonial cleansing, but the exemption from sin or to be considered innocent of something, thereby leaving one clean and pure. God prevented David from building His temple because he had dirty hands from shedding too much blood. Ceremonial washing could not remove David's tarnish; only God's forgiveness was adequate. This cleansing is available to all who confess their sins according to 1 John 1:9. The world needs more people with clean hands and pure hearts who will stand for justice, be merciful, and walk humbly with God. Would you be such a person?

Raise your hands confidently in gratitude and worship to God. Raising the hands in worship indicates the psychological, emotional, mental, and spiritual state of a worshipper. Successful athletes and powerful leaders exhibit the Victory Salute or the Power Posture – raising hands to express pride and power. Christians should consistently raise their hands because they share and desire more of God's power and victory over sin. May you follow scriptures examples of raising your hands in worship – 2 Chronicles 6:2, Ezra 9:5, Psalm 63:4, 134:2, and 1 Timothy 2:8.

Ralford Jones, Ed.D., Psy.D.

DEVOTIONAL REFLECTION

Give your feedback on the devotions relating to the hands.

_____

_____

_____

Are you comfortable waving your hands in church or public worship, to praise God?

_____

_____

_____

What comparison can you make between COVID – 19 and sin?

_____

_____

_____

How can you use your hands to safely touch someone you love?

_____

_____

_____

If you can play an instrument to praise God for your hands, what song would you choose and why?

_____

_____

_____

DAY 23

CHALLENGE YOUR HEART TO LOVE DEEPLY

"It's not the depth of your intellect that will comfort you or transform your world. Only the richness of your heart and your generosity of spirit can do that."
—Rasheed Ogunlaru

Ralford Jones, Ed.D., Psy.D.

BODY FACTS

The heart is a vital organ. It is responsible for nourishing the cells with energy, hormones, nutrients, and love. An average adult's heart beats approximately one hundred thousand times daily or about thirty-five million times yearly.

Imagine how intricate and vital your heart is, and lift your glass in gratitude to God for His genius design, creation, and functioning of your heart. "Trust in the LORD with all your heart and lean not on your own understanding; in all your ways submit to him, and he will make your paths straight." (Proverbs 3:5-6 NIV). **Be prepared for a four-day journey with the heart.**

CHALLENGE YOUR HEART
TO LOVE DEEPLY

"Jesus said unto him, Thou shalt love the Lord thy God with all thy heart, and with all thy soul, and with all thy mind" (Matthew 22:37 KJB).

Your heart is more than a pump! It is a machine that manufactures and disseminates love. God designed your heart to love Him passionately, consistently, and unconditionally. You can attain this love; it's uncomplicated, heart-warming, and seeks emotional involvement.

Loving God with all our hearts positions us to love our neighbors as ourselves. Matthew 23:37 (NIV) answers the rich young ruler's question: "What must I do to inherit eternal life?" Jesus's answer involves stretching the heart outside its comfort zone toward the love that resided in His heart. This expansion is possible with the Holy Spirit's assistance. This religious leader did not understand that loving God was associated with deep emotional involvement with others, even the poor.

The Holy Spirit can infuse deep love in our hearts for each other; Matthew 22:39 (NIV) shows us how. "Love your neighbor as yourself." The Bible presents the heart as an energetic, emotional, rational, and spiritual organ that is faithful, loyal, and cheerful; it also loves, trusts, thinks, deceives, praises, meditates, and serves. The heart can 'recklessly' and exuberantly love because of what it sees, feels, and desires.

After seeing each other on the street, two toddler friends ran excitedly and embraced lovingly and firmly, without considering the onlookers' thoughts or criticisms. No wonder this video went viral. If you saw Jesus coming toward you, how would you react?

Today, thank God with and for your heart! Love is God's operating system for our hearts – "Let all you do be done in love" (I Corinthians 16:14 KJV). Without love, our heart's rhythms are like a noisy gong or a banging cymbal. So, let your heartbeat flow with the beat on the drum, the guitar's strum, or nature's hum. May God's love saturate your heart always.

Ralford Jones, Ed.D., Psy.D.

DEVOTIONAL REFLECTION

What does it take to be deeply in love with God?

_____

_____

_____

Is there anything about your heart that fascinates you and prompts gratitude and obedience to God?

_____

_____

_____

How can you allow God to use your heart to honor Him and achieve His goals for your life?

_____

_____

_____

How does the physical condition of the heart affect one's spiritual functioning?

_____

_____

_____

Are you deeply in love with God? If yes, how do you know?

_____

_____

_____

VIGILANTLY PROTECT YOUR HEART

"Let my soul smile through my heart and my heart smile through my eyes, that I may scatter rich smiles in sad hearts."
—Paramahansa Yogananda

BODY FACTS

The heart is a major part of the circulatory system. It sends about five or six quarts of blood to the entire body in about twenty seconds. Approximately 20 percent of the blood goes to the kidney to be filtered, and 15 percent goes to the brain.

God deserves more appreciation, glory, and honor than customarily attributed to Him for creating our amazing hearts. Keeping your heart healthy is one way to glorify God for His genius creation.

VIGILANTLY PROTECT YOUR HEART

"Keep your heart with all vigilance, for from it flow the springs of life (Proverbs 4:23 ESV).

It is thinking on its own! Your heart can act independently from the brain. Don't be surprised that your heart has its nervous system.

God is very interested in the health status of our hearts. The imperative of Proverbs 4:23 implies that we should use the best resources: physician and medicine, motivation and attentiveness, social interactions and emotional regulations, rest and meditation, and scientific knowledge and spiritual practices to protect and cherish it. The focus and watchfulness implied by the text require 24-7 vigilance. So, during your sleeping hours, trust God to continue the vigil.

The heart is God's favorite hangout spot. Allowing God to reside inside you is a wise decision that results in restoration and protection. This decision is the most visionary cardiac plan and protocol because no one or nothing can protect our hearts like God. Accepting God as Lord and Savior of our lives opens the entrance of our hearts to Him. "I am crucified with Christ; and it is no longer I who live, but it is Christ who lives in me" (Galatians 2:20, NIV). According to Ephesians 3:17, Christ dwells in our hearts through faith.

Jeremiah 17:9 (NIV) shows why you should vigilantly watch your heart. "The heart is deceitful above all things and beyond cure. Who can understand it?" I Kings 8:39 mentions that only God knows our hearts. I Samuel 16:7 notes that humans look at the outside, but God sees the inside of the heart. According to Psalm 44:21, God knows the secret things of your heart.

Give gratitude to God for and with your heart. Imagine each heartbeat is a movement of praise to God. The electrical system of Adam's heart controlled its orderly rate and rhythms. Such coincided with nature's tempo – a worshipful pulsation to the Creator. May your heartbeat coincide with God's tempo.

Ralford Jones, Ed.D., Psy.D.

DEVOTIONAL REFLECTION

What is your understanding of Proverbs 4:23?

_____

_____

_____

What are the best practices to protect your heart?

_____

_____

_____

What are some creative ways to praise God with and for your heart?

_____

_____

_____

Are you concerned about someone with an unhealthy heart? What can you do to help?

_____

_____

_____

Is your heart getting adequate exercise?

_____

_____

_____

LET GOD TRANSFORM YOUR HEART

Keep your feet on the ground, but let your heart soar
as high as it will. Refuse to be average or to surrender
to the chill of your spiritual environment.
—Arthur Helps

Ralford Jones, Ed.D., Psy.D.

BODY FACTS

An average adult with a healthy heart will experience about seventy-two beats per minute. Every part of the body requires continuous nutrition to stay active; for this to happen, the heart must supply the needed blood for the survival of the entire body.

If you are counting your blessings and thanking God today, let the beating of your heart be included in that calculation.

LET GOD TRANSFORM YOUR HEART

*"I will give you a new heart and put a new spirit in you;
I will remove from you your heart of stone and give you a
heart of flesh" (Ezekiel 36:26 NIV).*

You might need a heart transplant! If your heart is spiritually cold or cynical toward God.

The message of Ezekiel 35:26 is redemptive and hopeful; it is something for which one's heart can skip a beat. A new heart allows us to share and receive love, forgiveness, and kindness at a high spiritual level. A new spirit shapes the personality so the selfish moods and attitudes can submit to God. The heart is unable to function well without a renewed spirit. The Israelites' sins corrupted and calcified their hearts; their sinful thoughts, emotions, and behaviors contributed to their disobedience, idolatry, rebelliousness, pride, and selfishness. Nevertheless, God made a covenant with them to renew their spirits and hearts. God can do the same for us today.

Spiritually, a new heart is a theoretical concept. If the heart's plan is radically contrary to the requirements of God's statutes and judgments, then a new heart is needed. God's laws reflect His priorities which He desires to download into our hearts. If the heart is disobedient to God's commandments, it becomes corrupt, carnal, and evil. Removal of these conditions can make the physical heart function more efficiently. This extraction is one of God's approaches to renew our hearts. The result is more godlike attitudes, new perspectives of righteousness, avoidance of old and new sinful ways, and increased willingness to submit to God's influence. Consequently, we become more emotionally connected to God and others.

Remember to let your heart rejoice in gratitude to God. Put a stethoscope over your heart and listen to its beating. Then be intentional to keep your heart healthy with exercise, diet, joy, laughter, love, positivity, prayer, relaxation, and sleep. May your heart beat in harmony with God's will always.

Ralford Jones, Ed.D., Psy.D.

DEVOTIONAL REFLECTION

What does it mean to you that God will give a new heart?

_____

_____

_____

What lifestyle change can you embrace to make your heart function more efficiently?

_____

_____

_____

Write a prayer of gratitude to God for the constant beating of your heart.

_____

_____

_____

If you have experienced a new heart, how is the experience impacting your life?

_____

_____

_____

What interests you about today's devotion?

_____

_____

_____

LIVING WITH A PURE HEART

"The Beatitudes are no spiritual "to do list" to be attempted by eager rule-keeping disciples. It is a spiritual "done" list of the qualities God brings to bear in the people who follow Jesus."
—Ronnie McBrayer

Ralford Jones, Ed.D., Psy.D.

BODY FACTS

The normal heart has of two sides. Each side has two chambers: an atrium and a ventricle. The atrium is called the upper chamber, and it collects blood that the kidney filtered and sends it to the ventricle or lower chamber, which pumps it to the rest of the body. Each chamber has two flaps that constantly open and close to enable blood flow in one direction.

Praise God for the functioning of your atria, ventricles, and kidneys.

LIVING WITH A PURE HEART

"Blessed are the pure in heart, for they will see God"
(Matthew 5:8 NIV).

A pure heart is real! It can fulfill God's utmost purpose for your life and help you to reside in His presence for eternity. Let your heart be excited because your best days are ahead.

In this beatitude, those with clean hearts receive the blessings of seeing God. Isaiah 7:4 predicted the birth of Jesus or Immanuel – "God with us." When Phillip asked Jesus to show him the Father, Jesus told his disciples that by seeing Him, they have seen the Father (John 14:8-9). With foresight and insights, we can see God in others.

Those with pure hearts will see God presently and in the future. As an everyday experience, we will recognize the blessings that surround us as rewards for our purity. We will also identify God's righteousness in ourselves and others. We can have clean hearts by accepting God's forgiveness and being obedient to the Holy Spirit. By imitating Christ's lifestyle, we also receive pure hearts. The spotless heart experience will enable us to see God in nature with new and fresh perspectives. Everywhere we go, it will be natural to see God in things, individuals, places, and situations.

As a future experience, those with clean hearts will see God forever. According to I Thessalonians 4:16-17, those who died with pure hearts will experience resurrection when Jesus returns. Let us encourage each other with this hopeful promise.

Think about your heart's work, then praise and glorify God's name. Imagine you went for a gratitude walk to increase your heart rate, and it extended to a longer happy run. The adrenalin continued rushing, so you went for a joy ride to tell a friend that Jesus rang your doorbell, walked in, took a towel, and cleaned your heart. Today, may you share the good news - your heart is Jesus's address.

Ralford Jones, Ed.D., Psy.D.

DEVOTIONAL REFLECTION

What do you think is the process for obtaining a pure heart?

_____

_____

_____

Your heart will help you to see God; what emotional reaction does this produce?

_____

_____

_____

Write a prayer to ask God for a pure heart.

_____

_____

_____

Can you envision your heart increasing its rhythm in gratitude to God?

_____

_____

_____

Are you excited that the pure heart will see God? What about this promise that gets you enthusiastic?

_____

_____

_____

WORSHIP GOD WITH YOUR STEADY WALK

"The human foot is a masterpiece of engineering and a work of art."
—Leonardo da Vinci

Ralford Jones, Ed.D., Psy.D.

BODY FACTS

The feet are the structures below the ankle – the heel, arch, and toes. They assist us in balancing and achieving extraordinary athletic feats.

The scientific information and mechanical functioning of the feet declare that God is a superb Designer, Engineer, and Creator. Our legs and feet can dance, jump, run, kick, stomp, and walk. You can use these activities to praise God. **The next two devotions are on the feet.**

WORSHIP GOD WITH
YOUR STEADY WALK

"My feet have closely followed his steps; I have kept to his way without turning aside" (Job 23:11 NIV).

Jump with excitement! If your walk with God is steady. Don't stumble into God's path because you will stray. But be intentional with your walk, and your feet will stay.

Job was a strict spiritual conformist who earned the highest divine admiration for his unique lifestyle. Job 23:11 provides an insight into Job's successful walk with God; Job was blameless, upright, and feared God. He shunned evil and lived a spiritually balanced and distinguished lifestyle. Job was deliberate and obedient: "I have not departed from the command of His lips; I have treasured the words of His mouth more than my daily bread" (Job 23:12 NIV).

Job's message connects with John 14:6 (NIV): "Jesus answered, 'I am the way, the truth, and the life. No one comes to the Father excepts through me.'" To walk closely in God's footprints, we must walk by and leap with faith. That was Job's experience, no wonder he operated on a different plane than all his contemporaries.

God is scouting for people like Job, who will demonstrate solid and progressive commitment in walking with Him. Some children play – *In the river on the bank.* Some adults are playing the game, but now, they are romping with their salvation. Job took his salvation seriously and placed his feet on solid ground. Psalm 1:1–3 declares that those who avoid walking with sinners, delight in God's law and meditate on them frequently, and will receive His blessings.

Praise God for and what your feet have contributed to your life. Let your feet worship God with holy dancing or walking (Psalm 149:3, Acts 3:8). Scientists found a pattern in nature that corresponds to musical rhythm. I pray that you will find your spiritual rhythm in your movements. May God sanctify your feet to worship Him daily.

Ralford Jones, Ed.D., Psy.D.

DEVOTIONAL REFLECTION

What are you willing to do to follow closely in Christ's steps?

_____

_____

_____

If you are very grateful to God for your feet, how can you show Him your gratitude?

_____

_____

_____

How steady is your walk with God?

_____

_____

_____

What are you doing with and for your feet to show God that you are taking good care of them?

_____

_____

_____

What's your view of Psalm 149:3 or using dancing in worship?

_____

_____

_____

BRINGING GOOD NEWS TO OTHERS

"God never said that the journey would be easy, but He did say that the arrival would be worthwhile."
—Max Lucado

BODY FACTS

Locomotion is the main reason for the feet. With the legs' assistance, the feet can climb, dance, drive, ride, ski, and complete other amazing feats.

Such agility is a blessing from God, for which He deserves all your praise, glory, honor, reverence, and respect. Keeping your feet healthy is one way to glorify God for them.

BRINGING GOOD NEWS TO OTHERS

"How beautiful upon the mountains are the feet of him who brings good news, who publishes peace, who brings good news of happiness, who publishes salvation, who says to Zion, Your God reigns" (Isaiah 52:7 ESV).

Some ugly feet are beautiful! With the proper mission, God can transform all feet into something attractive. God is enlisting runners to spread His good news of salvation, and the benefits are advantageous.

Isaiah's description of the feet is contradictory to our contemporary ideas of what defines beauty. Imagine someone in Isaiah's time, traveling barefooted or wearing uncomfortable footwear on rugged terrain, and long journeys to remote places. These experiences create ugly feet based on modern perceptions. However, it is not the conditions of the feet that make them beautiful but the passion, compassion, commission, and mission. Bringing the good news of happiness to those who have lost their joy due to depression, anxiety, fear, or hopelessness can create beautiful feet. When we are on God's mission and bring the Gospel of salvation to those who cannot see beyond the chaos of this world, our efforts can bring blessings to us and the receivers.

Paul, the apostle, traveled to many countries after God recruited him to spread the Gospel. In Romans 10:15 (NIV), Paul reiterated Isaiah's message: "How beautiful are the feet of those who bring good news." At the end of his challenging missions, Paul announced that he fought well, completed the race, was faithful to his mission, and expected a righteous crown from Jesus, along with those who love and anticipate His Second Coming (2 Timothy 4:7–8).

Are you worshiping God sufficiently for and with your feet? Imagine worshipping outside with a jump rope and music, where you will skip with nature's rhythm. This exercise can grow your brain, improve concentration and coordination. If your health doesn't allow this activity, visualize it and move to the praise beat. May you use your good fortune of healthy feet to praise God regularly.

Ralford Jones, Ed.D., Psy.D.

DEVOTIONAL REFLECTION

What is your definition of beautiful feet?

_____

_____

_____

How would God describe your feet right now?

_____

_____

_____

Are you using your feet to spread hope, peace, and the good news of salvation to others?

_____

_____

_____

Take some time to think of your feet and how they have impacted your life, and then write a note of gratitude to God for them.

_____

_____

_____

Are you flowing with God's rhythm for your feet?

_____

_____

_____

CREATED PERFECTLY

"The human body is the most complex system ever
created, the more we learn about it, the more appreciation
we have about what a rich system it is."
—Bill Gates

BODY FACTS

The body has more than twenty organs. The ten most popular listed ones are the brain, heart, kidney, large intestine, liver, lungs, pancreas, skin, small intestine, and stomach. The designs, locations, complexities, and orderly functioning of all the organs suggest that they were well thought out by a creative and Superior Intelligent Being.

Irrespective of the shape, size, color, height, and weight of your body, it is the best one you have; so, treat it with great care, love, respect, and reverence because you belong to the Lord (Psalm 24:24). Therefore, be generous with your praise to God for your body. Take the best care you can of your body and dedicate it entirely to God. Get excited, **here are the last three devotions – Created Perfectly, Made in God's Image, and Made for God's Glory.**

CREATED PERFECTLY

"I will praise You, for I am fearfully and wonderfully made. Marvelous are Your works, and I know this very well"
(Psalm 139:14 BSB).

Like water from a rushing torrent! Let your praises flow from different parts of your body in response to God's creative power and the fantastic functioning of your being.

David's declaration – "I am fearfully and wonderfully made," closely complements God's description of "very good," in Genesis 1:31. This description implies that Adam and Eve were the crème de la crème (best of the best) of creation. God used the highest-grade materials to create Adam. God also gave His most focused attention, tender loving care, and brilliant thoughts to make every fiber of Adam and Eve's bodies. God put a whole lot of love in creating the first couple.

Scientists assisted our understanding of God's description of "very good." By dividing the human body into twelve or more different systems that function interrelatedly. For example, the circulatory and cardiovascular systems work collaboratively with the heart, to transport disease-defense substances, hormones, nutrients, oxygen, and waste through and from the body.

God designed our bodies to miraculously heal themselves when they are bruised, cut, or broken. The healing process also occurs daily with new cell production; the liver is vital for these wonders. Our bodies use healthy foods to heal themselves; the intestines are essential for such functioning. The brain builds new neural connections, from which new cells emerge to create new neural pathways. The body also uses positive thoughts, love, faith, meditation, touch, and prayers to heal and restore itself constantly. The lungs can significantly repair themselves even when severely damaged after years of abuse.

Ralford Jones, Ed.D., Psy.D.

Get excited about your breathing system and praise God! Genesis 2:7 shows God sharing His breath (*nismat*), intellect, or spiritual essence with Adam. Breathing is our life-stream connection with God; it refreshes our relationship with Him. May you be one in spirit with Christ (I Corinthians 6:17), so your intentional breathing becomes a contentious worship experience.

Devotional Reflection

Are you fearfully and wonderfully made? If yes, please explain.

_____

_____

_____

Do you think God is satisfied with how much you praise Him for creating you?

_____

_____

_____

Does your praise involve mentioning specific body parts?

_____

_____

_____

Are you praising God by the way you care for your body?

_____

_____

_____

Write any additional comments you have about today's devotion.

_____

_____

_____

Ralford Jones, Ed.D., Psy.D.

MADE IN GOD'S IMAGE

"The human body is comprised of an amalgamation of different systems that together make a complex organism that exhibits symmetry and order. The aforementioned function of the brain and the nervous system exhibit a symmetry and complexity that warrants a belief in a grand designer."
—Jacob H. Rhodes

Ralford Jones, Ed.D., Psy.D.

BODY FACTS

Metabolism is one of the great functions of the human body. It is the life-sustaining biochemical process that involves the breakdown and buildup of substances in the body. The metabolic process also controls body weight, food digestion, brain and heart functions, growth, damage repair, energy production, waste elimination, and breathing.

The olfactory system consists of the nose and the nasal cavities. This sensory system is vital for breathing and smelling. Inhalation stimulates the amygdala and hypothalamus, the areas of the brain that influence our emotions. Give God a big THANK YOU for your metabolic and olfactory systems.

MADE IN GOD'S IMAGE

"And God said, let us make man in our image, after our likeness: and let them have dominion over the earth. . ." (Genesis 1:26 NIV).

You are not here by accident! God knew you before your birth – (Psalm 139:15,16, and Galatians 1:15). God created you in His image for a purpose.

There is more than one biblical Hebrew word for 'image' and 'likeness.' The word in the main text is *tselem*, meaning shadow. Adam was an outline shadow or shape of God. *Pesel* means to carve out an image of something seen. *Demut* denotes resemblance or likeness in appearance, like a son who shows his biological father's similarity. *Temunah* means likeness. In the decalogue – Exodus 20:4, God commanded the Israelites not to make any image (*pesel*) or likeness of the things in heaven and earth. In biblical Greek, *eiko* and *eikon* suggest that Christ resembles or is God's very image (2 Corinthians 4:4 and Colossians 1:15). According to the Merriam-Webster Dictionary, an image represents an object like a photograph of someone on television.

The meaning of God's image or the Imago Dei has two main interpretations by theologians. One belief is that God has physical human-like features that He attributed to Adam and Eve. Another variation is that the words "likeness" and "image" refer to God's essence as a spiritual, moral, and powerful being who attributed these qualities to our forebears. God is invisible, yet has an image (*eikon*) – Colossians 1:15. God can assume different forms and likenesses; this is His prerogative. God chose to create Adam in His human likeness.

Thank God for your nose and worship Him with your breathing. The Hebrew words for breath are **Nismat** and *ruakh* (wind, Spirit). The Greek word *pneuma* means breath and Spirit. Job believed that God's Spirit (*ruakh*) – breathed and resided in his nostrils (Job 27:3). Don't just breathe automatically; respire with awareness like Job. May this conscious effort reduce your anxiety, improve your concentration, and glorify God.

Ralford Jones, Ed.D., Psy.D.

DEVOTIONAL REFLECTION

What does it mean to be created in the image and likeness of God?

_____

_____

_____

Which part of your body's design fascinates you the most and why?

_____

_____

_____

What can you do to manifest God's likeness?

_____

_____

_____

Write a short prayer of gratitude to God for creating you in His image and likeness.

_____

_____

_____

What is your understanding of Genesis 2:7?

_____

_____

_____

MADE FOR GOD'S GLORY

"The human body is capable of amazing physical deeds. If we
could just free ourselves from our perceived limitations and
tap into our internal fire, the possibilities are endless."
—Dean Karnazes

"I will attach tendons to you and make flesh
come upon you and cover you with skin;
I will put breath in you, and you will come to life.
Then you will know that I am the LORD"
–Ezekiel 37:6 (NIV).

Ralford Jones, Ed.D., Psy.D.

BODY FACTS

The skin is our biggest organ, weighing about 8 pounds for many adults. Our skin protects us from the sun, dangerous microbes, and harmful chemicals. It also manufactures vitamin D.

The skin can absorb and radiate God's glory visibly. When Moses came down from Mount Sinai after meeting God, his face shone according to Exodus 34:29. Proper breathing can cause your skin to look healthy.

MADE FOR GOD'S GLORY

"Bring all who claim me as their God, for I have made them for my glory. It was I who created them." (Isaiah 46:7 NLT)

This is the best thing that could ever happen to you! That is, living a purposeful life that focuses on glorifying God. Living otherwise is wasteful.

Isaiah 46:7 presents three ideas: God created us all for the same purpose, claiming God brings privileges, and God's proprietorship is a unique prerogative that He asserts. God was not on a power trip when He created us for His glory. The text shows human choice, not manipulation. Corresponding texts reveal that God created us to share His image, likeness, authority, and glory.

God's glory is His magnificent presence; He does not share this grandeur with other gods (Isaiah 42:8). Revelation 21:11 describes God's glory as radiance, like a rare jewel of glistening stones. According to Exodus 24:17, the glory of God appeared as a devouring fire, and Exodus 13:21 (NIV) calls it a pillar of fire. "By day the LORD went ahead. . . by night in a pillar of fire to give them light, so that they could travel by day or night." God made us so we can experience His glory. He is an involved Creator; His constant presence guides, provides, and protects.

Another aspect of God's glory is His name, according to Psalm 72:19 (NLT). "Praise his glorious name forever! Let the whole earth be filled with his glory. . ." Isaiah 43:21 (NIV) reiterates that God made us to praise Him – "The people I formed for myself that they may proclaim my praise."

Today, glorify God for and with your nostrils. Practice **Power Breathing** – simultaneous prayer and deep breathing. An example is a one-breath prayer – *God, use my breath to refresh my stale faith*, then exhale. Imagine you inhaled and the oxygen oxidizes your sinful thoughts; then you exhaled and removed the waste – carbon dioxide, malice, and unforgiveness. May your nostrils be the Holy Spirit's address.

Ralford Jones, Ed.D., Psy.D.

DEVOTIONAL REFLECTION

Do you have additional information about God's glory than what is given in the devotion?

_____

_____

_____

How can God's glory be shared with us?

_____

_____

_____

Are you living up to God's expectations relating to glorifying His name?

_____

_____

_____

Read Exodus 33:22-34:8 and share your thoughts.

_____

_____

_____

What are your opinions about praising and thanking God for the design and creation of your different body parts and to use them for such expressions?

_____

_____

_____